F HORN

FOR CHURCH

AMY ADAM
MIKE HANNICKEL

Edition Number: CMP 0873.03

Amy Adam, Mike Hannickel
TONS OF TUNES for Church
F Horn

ISBN 90-431-1978-4

CD number: 19.047-3 CMP
CD arrangements by James L. Hosay

© Copyright 2003 by Curnow Music Press, Inc.
P.O. Box 142, Wilmore KY 40390, USA

ARRANGERS

MIKE HANNICKEL grew up in the Sacramento, California area and attended California State University, Sacramento and the University of Southern California. He has been a music teacher In Rocklin, California since 1973. He also composes and publishes exclusively with Curnow Music Press, with whom he has dozens of pieces of music in print.

AMY ADAM was raised in Grand Rapids, Minnesota and attended the University of Minnesota, Duluth graduating with a BM in band education and Flute performance. She has been a music teacher in California since 1992 and currently teaches in Rocklin, California.

TONS OF TUNES

TONS OF TUNES FOR CHURCH is filled with fun and familiar pieces that musicians love to play. All the songs have been arranged in easy keys for wind instruments. The **professional quality accompaniment CD** can be used for practice and performance. You may also choose to purchase the separately available Piano accompaniment part.

TO THE MUSIC TEACHER OR CHURCH MUSIC DIRECTOR:
TONS OF TUNES for CHURCH is a great way to help get young musicians actively involved in your church music program. Every tune in the book can be performed with the included CD accompaniment or with the separately available Piano/Organ book. All **TONS OF TUNES for CHURCH** books can be used alone or together so a variety of small ensembles can be created. Whether for prelude, offertory, church social, talent show or any other gathering, **TONS OF TUNES for CHURCH** is just what you need. Chord symbols are provided in the Piano accompaniment book for Keyboard, Guitar and combo use.

TO THE MUSICIAN:
Have **FUN** playing these songs alone or with your family and friends! Even if you have different instruments, you can still play together. Each person needs to get the **TONS OF TUNES FOR CHURCH** book for their instrument.

FOR CHURCH
CONTENTS

TRACK		PAGE
1	Tuning Note E	
2	Tuning Note F	
3	1. Abide With Me	5
4	2. Now Thank We All Our God	5
5	3. Do, Lord	6
6	4. Beautiful Savior	6
7	5. For the Beauty of the Earth	7
8	6. Holy, Holy, Holy	7
9	7. Jesus Loves Me	8
10	8. My Faith Looks Up to Thee	8
11	9. Just As I Am	9
12	10. Crown Him With Many Crowns	9
13	11. Come, Thou Almighty King	10
14	12. Oh, Won't You Sit Down?	10
15	13. O For a Thousand Tongues	11
16	14. Children of the Heavenly Father	11
17	15. The Church's One Foundation	12
18	16. Nearer My God to Thee	12
19	17. Praise to the Lord, the Almighty	13
20	18. All Glory, Laud and Honor	13
21	19. All Hail the Power	14
22	20. God of Grace and God of Glory	14
23	21. Swing Low, Sweet Chariot	15
24	22. He's Got the Whole World in His Hands	15
25	23. Go Tell it on the Mountain	16
26	24. This Train	16
27	25. What a Friend we have in Jesus	17
28	26. Onward Christian Soldiers	17
29	27. In the Sweet By and By	18
30	28. Let Us Break Bread Together	18
31	29. Christ the Lord is Risen Today	19
32	30. Were You There?	19
33	31. This is my Father's World	20
34	32. Softly and Tenderly Jesus is Calling	20

TONS OF TUNES FOR CHURCH

Amy Adam (ASCAP) and
Mike Hannickel (ASCAP)

1. ABIDE WITH ME

TRACK 3

2. NOW THANK WE ALL OUR GOD

TRACK 4

5. FOR THE BEAUTY OF THE EARTH

6. HOLY, HOLY, HOLY

7. JESUS LOVES ME

8. MY FAITH LOOKS UP TO THEE

9. JUST AS I AM

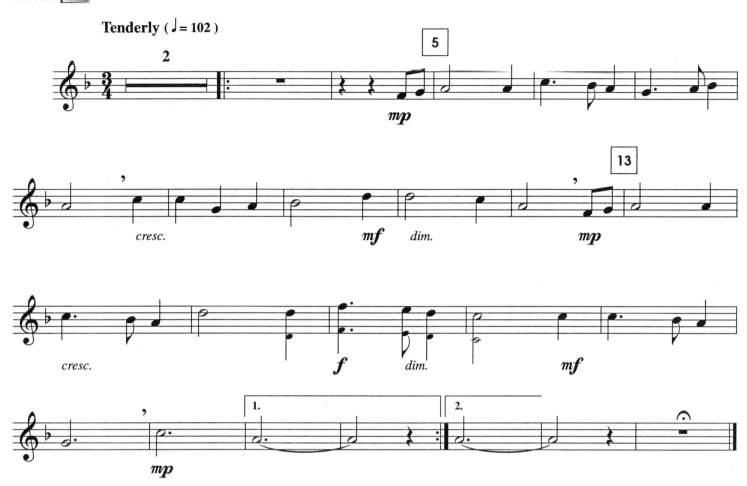

10. CROWN HIM WITH MANY CROWNS

11. COME, THOU ALMIGHTY KING

Moderately (♩ = 112)

12. OH, WON'T YOU SIT DOWN?

Swing (♩ = 144)

0873.03 CMP • F Horn

13. O FOR A THOUSAND TONGUES

14. CHILDREN OF THE HEAVENLY FATHER

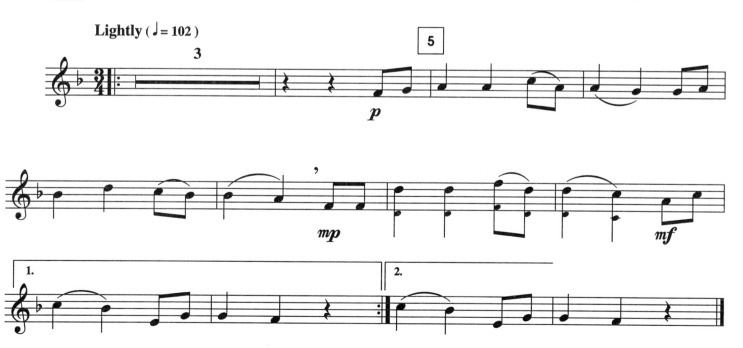

15. THE CHURCH'S ONE FOUNDATION

16. NEARER MY GOD TO THEE

17. PRAISE TO THE LORD, THE ALMIGHTY

18. ALL GLORY, LAUD AND HONOR

19. ALL HAIL THE POWER

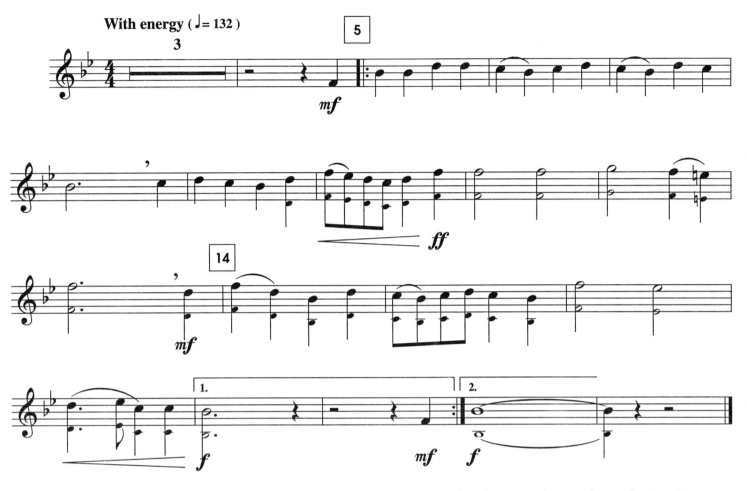

20. GOD OF GRACE AND GOD OF GLORY

21. SWING LOW, SWEET CHARIOT

22. HE'S GOT THE WHOLE WORLD IN HIS HANDS

Swing (♩ = 124)

23. GO TELL IT ON THE MOUNTAIN

24. THIS TRAIN

25. WHAT A FRIEND WE HAVE IN JESUS

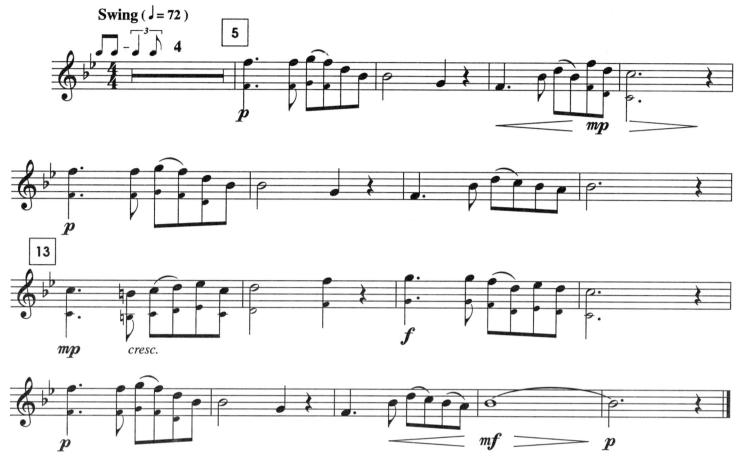

26. ONWARD CHRISTIAN SOLDIERS

27. IN THE SWEET BY AND BY

28. LET US BREAK BREAD TOGETHER

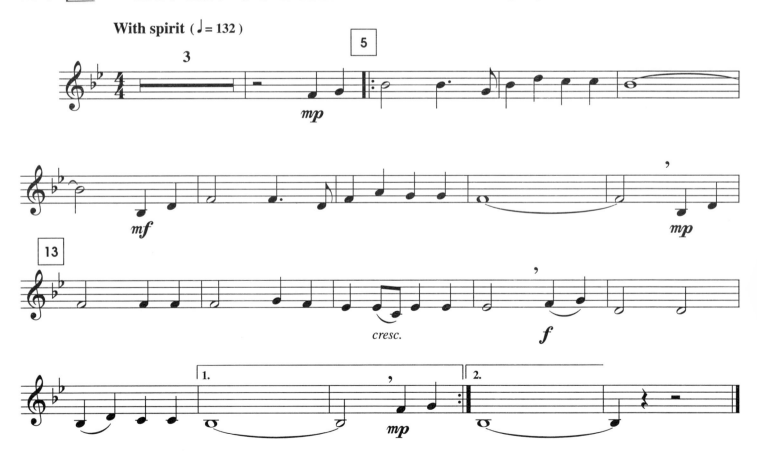

29. CHRIST THE LORD IS RISEN TODAY

30. WERE YOU THERE?

31. THIS IS MY FATHER'S WORLD

32. SOFTLY AND TENDERLY JESUS IS CALLING

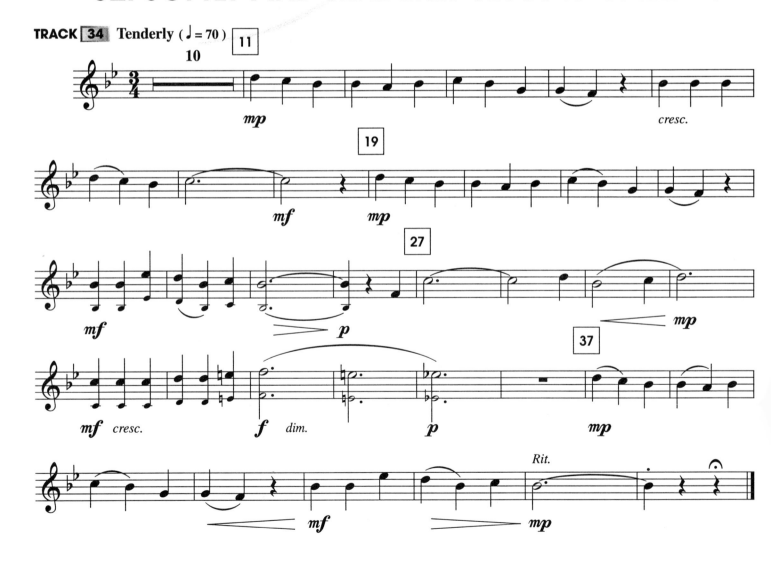